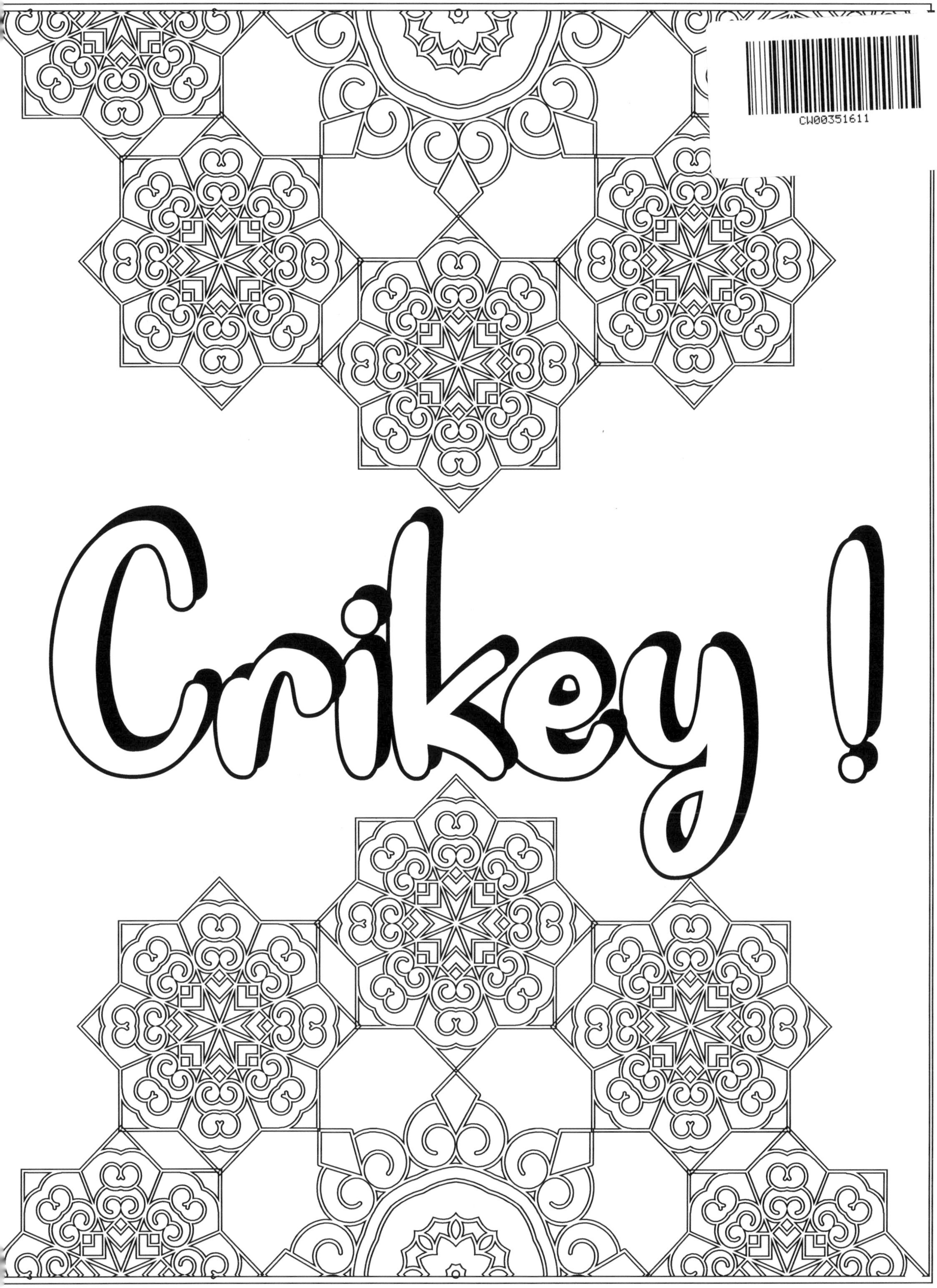
Crikey !

Fudge

Geez
Louise

Holy moly !

What the WHAT!

Shut The front door !

Sugar
Honey
Ice tea !

Cheeses !

Son of baptist!

fiddlesticks!

dagnamit!

Gadzooks !

oh for pete's sake !

Darn!

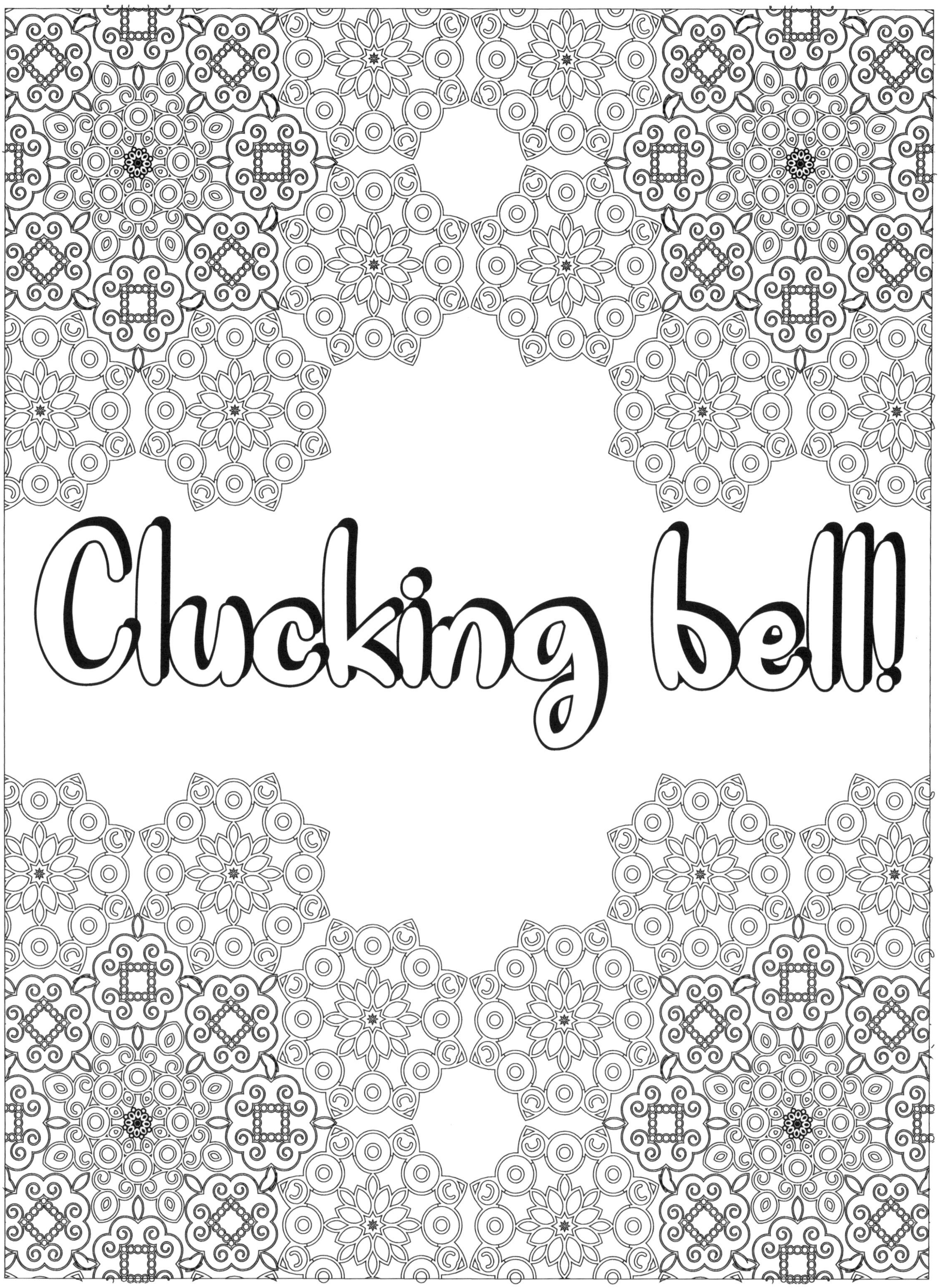
Clucking bell!

Shiitake mushrooms!

Printed in Great Britain
by Amazon

10241469R00020